Friends, Bullies and Staying Safe

Friends, Bullies and Staying Safe

The Adoption Club Therapeutic Workbook on Friendship

Regina M. Kupecky

Illustrated by Apsley

Jessica Kingsley *Publishers*
London and Philadelphia

First published in 2015
by Jessica Kingsley Publishers
73 Collier Street
London N1 9BE, UK
and
400 Market Street, Suite 400
Philadelphia, PA 19106, USA

www.jkp.com

Copyright © Regina M. Kupecky 2015
Illustrations copyright © Apsley 2015

Library of Congress Cataloging in Publication Data
A CIP catalog record for this book is available from the Library of Congress

British Library Cataloguing in Publication Data
A CIP catalogue record for this book is available from the British Library

ISBN 978 1 84905 763 9
eISBN 978 0 85700 994 4

Printed and bound in Great Britain

INTRODUCTION FOR ADULTS

About this series

This workbook is Book 4 of a series of workbooks about The Adoption Club written for counselors or therapists working with children aged 5–11, as well as adoptive parents.

The five interactive therapeutic workbooks have been written to address the key emotional and psychological challenges they are likely to experience. They provide an approachable, interactive and playful way to help children to learn about themselves and have fun at the same time.

About this book

Friends, Bullies and Staying Safe is the fourth book in the Adoption Club series and introduces friendships, teasing and ways to cope with bullies.

It is difficult for many children to know the difference between casual and close friends. Some adopted children try to control others as a result of their past life.

Whether you are a parent, a counselor, a therapist, a social worker or a doctor this book will help children by opening up discussion about friendship. They will no longer feel alone, because they can find a character whose story resembles theirs.

The story brings up many topics, and completing the workbook will probably take many sessions. The coloring and workbook format helps children express their own feelings in a non-threatening way. Helping them make their own friendship target will teach them the differences between different kinds of friends.

Hopefully, the workbook will help the child discuss peers in a healthy way.

If you have questions or need help please drop me an email at ReginaKu@msn.com

Other workbooks in the Adoption Club series

Book 1: *Let's Learn About Adoption: The Adoption Club Therapeutic Workbook on Adoption and Its Many Different Forms*

Book 2: *How Do We Feel About Adoption? The Adoption Club Therapeutic Workbook on Feelings and Behavior*

Book 3: *The Confusing World of Brothers, Sisters and Adoption: The Adoption Club Therapeutic Workbook on Siblings*

Book 5: *Who We Are and Why We Are Special: The Adoption Club Therapeutic Workbook on Identity*

Meet The Adoption Club!

The Adoption Club is made up of many characters whose lives have been touched by adoption.

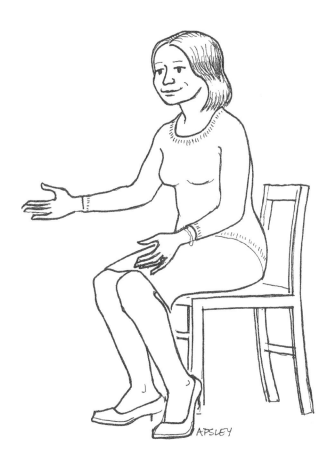

Mrs. Bright is the counselor who runs the group.

Mr. Jackman is a history teacher who helps. He was adopted as an infant in a closed adoption. That meant growing up he knew nothing about his birth parents. As an adult he searched for them and found them.

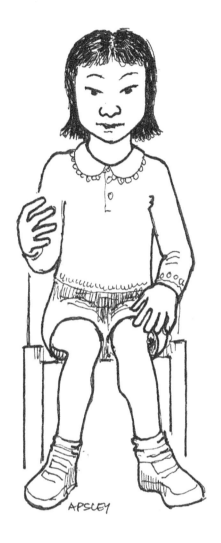

Mary was adopted from China by her single mom. Everyone knows she is adopted because her mom is White and she is Asian. She was three years old when she came to her mom. She is ten right now. She was left by her birth family near the post office in China and then went to an orphanage.

Alexander was adopted from Russia by a single dad. He was five when he joined his family. He lived in an orphanage too.

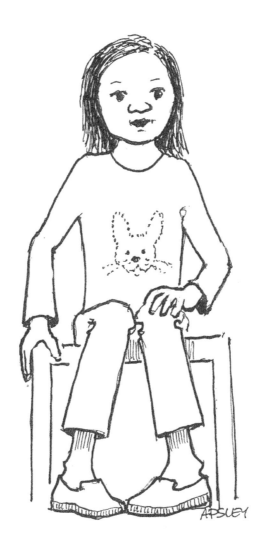

Alice was adopted in an open adoption as an infant. Her birth mother is of Mexican heritage and her birth father is of Puerto Rican heritage. Her birth parents chose her adoptive parents. She still visits her birth parents. She is nine and has one brother who was born to her adoptive parents.

Angela is nine and her birth brother Michael is thirteen. They lived with their birth parents for many years until they went into foster care. Both lived in several homes, and not always together. They have been in their adoptive family for one year. The family adopted two other children before them, who are now four and six.

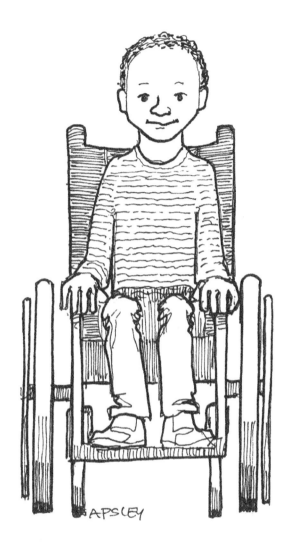

Robert has a disability and needs a wheelchair to get around.
He is twelve and was adopted into a kinship adoption, which
means he is related to his adoptive family. His adoptive mom
is his birth father's sister. They have four birth children and
may adopt again. It is a big family.

Friends, Bullies and Staying Safe

Mr. Jackman arranged the chairs for the meeting of The Adoption Club. Being adopted himself, he enjoyed helping the members talk about topics that interested them. He taught history in the school and often commented in class about famous historical characters who were adopted. He wanted to let other adoptees know that being adopted is part of who they are, but not all of who they are.

Mrs. Bright came in. She was the school counselor. She, her husband and Mr. Jackman were friends as well as fellow employees. Her husband and Mr. Jackman both enjoyed golf, and the three of them often went to see plays together.

Tonight, the topic was friendship and they were both interested in what the children had to say.

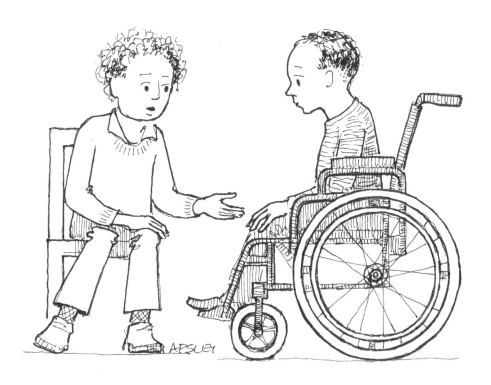

Before long, all the children had arrived. They sat in their seats and began to talk and laugh.

Mr. Jackman said, "Do you consider yourselves friends?"

The children all looked at each other.

"I guess so," said Alexander. "We go to the same school and belong to The Adoption Club."

Robert said, "Well, besides this, Alexander and I go to the same church so we see each other there."

Michael said, with a nod to Angela, "She is my sister, but siblings aren't friends, are they?"

Alice and Mary joined in the laughter.

Can siblings be friends?

_____

_____

_____

_____

_____

Mrs. Bright smiled. "There are all kinds of friendships," she said.

She drew a large target on a piece of paper.

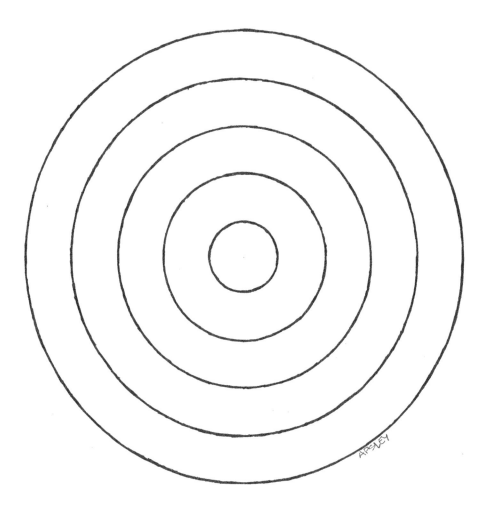

She started with the outer circle. "These people we may see often—we are polite, but do not share activities or serious conversation. For me, it is the people at the coffee shop. I say hello and know their first names, but I know nothing about their personal lives, or even their last names."

"Oh," said Alice, "like the older lady I see on the way to school. She walks her dog. I say hello and pet the dog, but I really do not know anything about her."

Mary chimed in, "I see the same mothers when I go to dance class. They are leaving with the younger children. Sometimes, I hold the door for them, and everyone smiles and says hello."

"Right," said Mr. Jackman. "These people are in and around our lives but are not really our friends."

Can you think of people who are on this level with you?

"The next circle is made up of people with whom we share part of our lives," Mrs. Bright continued.

"For example, other students in your class may belong to this circle. You may do a project together, share art supplies, help them with homework or other chores in the classroom. But you do not call them, text them, go to their house, or share private thoughts with them. You may play on the playground with them in a group, but you do not tell them your feelings and you probably don't tell them your history."

"I never tell those kids that I am adopted," said Michael. "They can be fun. Sometimes they might tease me, but they are mostly OK."

Mary made a face. "Since I am Asian and my mom isn't, everyone knows I am adopted. Sometimes kids who know me at this level tease me about my birth parents, adoption or my race. I never know what to say to stop it."

Do you ever tease children who are different?

_____

_____

_____

_____

Do you ever get teased?

_____

_____

_____

_____

_____

_____

_____

_____

_____

_____

Alexander nodded. "Mary," he said, "before The Adoption Club, I was a friend with you on that level. I knew you were adopted but never told you I was adopted too. I never teased you though. Since we have been meeting and sharing thoughts and feelings, I think we have moved up a level. We know each other better."

Mary agreed.

How can you move from one level to the next?

_____

_____

_____

_____

_____

_____

Have you ever done that?

_____

_____

_____

_____

_____

_____

_____

"You move levels by being closer. You children have shared thoughts and feelings about adoption at the club. You have also learned to trust each other. You don't tell the other children what we talk about here. Trust and sharing are how we get closer," said Mr. Jackman.

Do you have friends you trust with your feelings?

Mrs. Bright asked, "What can you do when being teased about adoption?"

Mary said, "I usually just say, 'You don't know what you are talking about' and walk away."

Alice said, "Some kids ask if I am going to find my real mom. They don't understand I see my birth mother regularly. I don't need to find her, I know where she is, but I don't tell them that."

Angela said, "My brother and I were older when we were adopted so some of the kids know. One minute my parents had no children, the next, they had two."

Everyone laughed.

She continued. "When they ask me things I don't want to discuss I just say I don't want to talk about it. When I refuse to answer, they are usually quiet.

"One girl, though, asks me something every day. She is very annoying and I finally told her to stop talking to me. It didn't work. Every day she asks, 'Why were you adopted?' and 'Where are your birth parents?'"

Do you have any ideas on what Angela should do?

_____

_____

_____

_____

_____

_____

_____

Has something like that ever happened to you?

_____

_____

_____

_____

_____

_____

_____

"I think," said Alice, "that you should talk to your parents about what to do."

"I would want to punch her," said Michael, "but I know that is not OK."

Robert looked thoughtful. "I wonder why she is so interested. Maybe you could ask her. Someone used to do that to me about my disability. When I asked him it turned out his cousin had the same disability, and he wanted information. Once he told me that, his questions were not so annoying."

Alexander laughed, "Maybe you should make up a list of books about adoption and hand it to her."

How do you handle teasing about adoption?

_____

_____

_____

_____

_____

_____

APSLEY

The children went around the circle.

"I," said Alexander, "try to educate. I tell them I was adopted from Russia, and that I am not going to live there again. Maybe visit. This is my family now and it will be until I am 100."

Michael said, "I change the subject. If they keep asking, I just walk away."

Angela said, "I tell them I don't discuss my adoption with anyone except my parents."

Mary said, "I say, 'Why do you want to know?' I put it back on them."

Robert said, "I just say I live with my aunt and uncle; they adopted me, so now they are my mom and dad."

Alice said, "I say my brother was born to my parents and I was adopted. It is the way it is in my family. No big deal."

What have you said or done when teased about adoption?

_____

_____

_____

_____

_____

_____

_____

Mrs. Bright held up the chart again.

"The next level is people with whom you may share a hobby or sport. You may see them every week at dance class, football practice, Boy Scouts or church. You may become closer by sharing texts, play dates or other activities as well. As you share more, you may get closer."

Do you have friends like this?

_____

_____

_____

_____

_____

_____

"Other friends come and go. You might be best friends one year and then one person moves and you never see them again. Losses like that are hard sometimes, but they are part of life."

How many friends do you have like this?

_____

_____

_____

_____

_____

_____

Mr. Jackman said, "The littlest circle is close friends. Most people have only a few close friends. They are the friends who you call when you need help. You share your feelings, joys, sorrows and thoughts with them. Sometimes, you might not see them for years, but when you do, it is like you never were apart. You might talk to them about your feelings about adoption."

Do you have a friend like that?

_____

_____

_____

_____

_____

Can you talk about adoption with them?

_____

_____

_____

_____

_____

"Time for a break," said Mr. Jackman.

After cookies and juice, the children came back together.

"I noticed," said Mrs. Bright, "that at break you divided up. Angela and Mary were talking."

"Right," said Mary. "We were talking about that new singer we like."

Michael rolled his eyes. "And Alexander and I were talking about the football game on Saturday. He invited me over to watch it with him. I am going to ask my mom if that is OK."

Robert and Alice laughed. "We were talking about a movie we both saw."

Mrs. Bright said, "You are all friends now, and sharing with people about the same topics or interests."

How else can you be a friend? Do you have some ideas?

_____

_____

_____

_____

_____

_____

_____

_____

_____

_____

"To be a friend you have to take turns," said Mary. "One of my friends loves to play board games. I prefer card games but we take turns playing what the other wants."

"You can't be bossy," said Alice. "You can't always be the leader, pick the game or be the first to do something. Even if you are better than your friend, you need to give everyone a chance."

Robert said, "My friends understand I can't play games that are running games. They play things I can play too. I also need to go to their football or track events even though I do not participate. I can cheer them on. One of my friends always comes to the events I can do."

Michael said, "There is something that is hard for me. I have a temper and sometimes I get too mad. I need to apologize after that and take responsibility. I am working on it, but it is hard for me."

Being a good friend is important if you want to make and keep friends. What do you do to make friends?

_____

_____

_____

_____

_____

What is hard for you?

_____

_____

_____

_____

_____

_____

_____

_____

"It was hard when we moved over and over again," said Angela. "When we first came to the family, I didn't want to make friends. I felt I would move again and lose them. I had to get closer to my mom and dad before I could trust I was staying somewhere and make friends."

Alexander nodded. "I guess my adoption feelings do affect other parts of my life. When I moved from the orphanage, I didn't speak English. I left all my orphanage friends behind. It was hard at first learning to play with friends in a new way and in a new language. In the orphanage friends were always there. But when they live in a family, they go home."

Robert said, "My adopted brothers and sisters all had friends. It took me a while to get used to a family and make friends. We are a big family and so everyone can't have friends over at the same time. Some kids don't want to be friends because of my medical issues." He pointed to his wheelchair. "It's not like they will catch my medical problem. But other kids are nice to me. Like you guys."

Do you think being adopted can affect your friendships?

_____

_____

_____

_____

Alice laughed. "And sometimes you need to go away. When my brother has a friend over sometimes they include me and sometimes they want to do something without me. I need to find something to do and leave them alone so I am not a pest."

Michael poked Angela. "Yes, sometimes younger sisters can be pests."

Do you have friends or a brother or sister who can be annoying?

_____

_____

_____

_____

_____

Do you ever think you can be annoying too?

_____

_____

_____

_____

_____

Mrs. Bright passed out copies of the circles. She asked each child to fill in the types of friends that they discussed.

Where on the circle would you put your different types of friends?

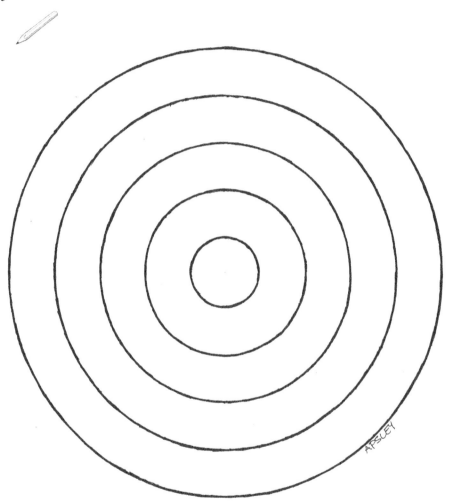

Where would you put each of your siblings?

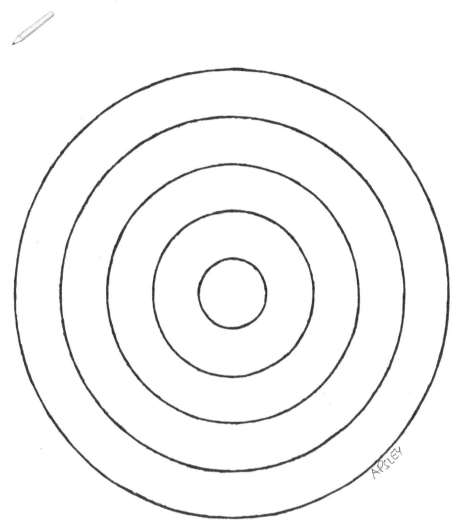

Mrs. Bright helped them share their circles. "Remember, you have to be a good friend too. That means you share."

"Don't be bossy," said Alice.

"Don't tell their secrets to other kids," said Robert.

"Don't tease them about adoption or how they look," said Mary.

"Don't get so mad at them," said Michael.

"Let other people, even your brother, have friends without you interfering," said Angela.

"Be a good friend if you want to have friends. Sometimes, do what they want to do," said Alexander.

"And remember," Mr. Jackman said, "friends can sometimes come and go, but your adoptive family is your family forever."

RESOURCES

Your child might enjoy

Brodzinsky, Anne Braff (2013) *Can I tell you about Adoption?* London, UK: Jessica Kingsley Publishers.

Schab, Lisa M., LCSW (2009) *Cool, Calm, and Confident: A Workbook to Help Kids Learn Assertiveness Skills.* Oakland, CA: Instant Help Books.

Schoettle, Marilyn (2000) *W.I.S.E. Up! Powerbook.* Burtonsville, MD: Center for Adoption Support and Education.

Shapiro, Lawrence, PhD (2008) *Let's Be Friends: A Workbook to Help Kids Learn Social Skills and Make Great Friends.* Oakland, CA: Instant Help Books.

Adults might enjoy

Kupecky, Regina and Keck, Gregory (1995) *Adopting the Hurt Child.* Colorado Springs, CO: Piñon Press.

Kupecky, Regina and Keck, Gregory (2002) *Parenting the Hurt Child.* Colorado Springs, CO: NavPress.

Madorsky Elman, Natalie and Kennedy-Moore, Eileen (2003) *The Unwritten Rules of Friendship: Simple Strategies to Help Your Child Make Friends.* New York, NY: Little, Brown and Company.

Thompson, Michael, Cohen, Lawrence J. and O'Neill Grace, Catherine (2004) *Mom, They're Teasing Me: Helping Your Child Solve Social Problems.* New York, NY: Ballantine Books.

CPI Antony Rowe
Eastbourne, UK
March 15, 2022